the
GREAT
STONE FACE

For Donald R. Hettinga,
a likeness of the Great Stone Face
— *G. D. S.*

To my wife, Deborah,
and my daughters, Allison and Caitlin
— *B. F.*

Text © 2002 Gary D. Schmidt
Illustrations © 2002 Bill Farnsworth

Published 2002 by Eerdmans Books for Young Readers
An imprint of Wm. B. Eerdmans Publishing Company
255 Jefferson S.E., Grand Rapids, Michigan 49503
P.O. Box 163, Cambridge CB39PU U.K.

ISBN 0-8028-5194-0 (cloth: alk. paper)
ISBN 0-8028-5292-0 (paper: alk. paper)

Library of Congress Cataloging-in-Publication Data
Schmidt, Gary D.
The Great Stone Face : a retelling of a tale by Nathaniel Hawthorne /
retold by Gary Schmidt ; illustrated by Bill Farnsworth.
p. cm.
Summary: As the years pass and his small village grows, Ethan watches for the
fulfullment of the prophecy that someone born looking like the Great Stone Face up on
the mountain will be the greatest, noblest person of his time.
[1. Prophecies—Fiction.] I. Hawthorne, Mathaniel, 1804 - 1864. II. Farnsworth, Bill, ill. III. Title.

PZ7.S3527 Gr 2002
[Fic]—dc21
2002021607

The illustrations were rendered in oils on canvas.
The display type was set in Prose Antiqua.
The text type was set in Schneidler.

the GREAT STONE FACE

A tale by

NATHANIEL HAWTHORNE

retold by

GARY D. SCHMIDT

illustrated by

BILL FARNSWORTH

EERDMANS BOOKS FOR YOUNG READERS

Grand Rapids, Michigan   Cambridge, U.K.

As long as New Hampshire eyes had looked up to the mountains, the Great Stone Face had stared back down in stony thought. And no one's eyes had looked up more than those of Ethan.

He could imagine the stone eyelids opening and the two granite lips parting to call out with thunder accents. Sometimes he clapped his hands to his ears as though the lips had already parted. Sometimes he waved a shy greeting as if the eyes had already opened.

On this day, the wind was rushing down from the Face, flashing the maples to gold and pushing Ethan back into the village. Hardly a village, really — more a collection of frame houses. One last gust and Ethan hunched his coat around himself and looked back over his shoulder.

"Are you watching then, just like him?" Pastor Hooper came out from his own afternoon walk.

"Him?"

"The Great Stone Face." The pastor turned to the Face that glowed in the lowering sun. "With the light just so, he seems to watch. You know the prophecy?"

Ethan nodded. "Someone will be born hereabouts who will look just like the Great Stone Face, and he will be the noblest person of his time. But no one believes it anymore."

"Count me as one of the believers," said Pastor Hooper and passed on into the village.

The very next day, news came that Augustus McBride was returning to town. Before Ethan was born, he had left to seek out his fortune, and now his bulky-bottomed ships filled warehouses from Boston to Bath with furs skinned from the Arctic, ivory culled from Africa, whale oil harpooned from all the seas of the earth.

And more astonishing still, it was said that the face of Augustus McBride was the very image of the Great Stone Face.

Augustus McBride sent a skilled and clever architect to build a proper mansion to hold him. In the freezing short days of January, February, and March, a palace fit for the Mediterannean rose up. Its marble was white as sugar. Tall columns spiraled down to a door fashioned with tropical woods, and the beveled glass of the windows prismed the light. The gleaming gold of the bedroom alone could blind the eye.

None of the villagers doubted that the prophecy would come true at last.

Just as the orchards started to bud, the great man came. Ethan waited on the Common to see him. Though the sun shone warmly, he shivered with the thrill and could not help but glance often at the Great Stone Face that watched so thoughtfully. He felt the granite smile break upon the village, and he knew it must be for Augustus McBride.

The rumble of wheels. The snorting of horses. "Here he comes!" cried a boy on the edge of the village. "Augustus McBride himself!"

The villagers pressed forward, Ethan with them, as a carriage rushed up to the Common. The driver reared the horses to a halt, and Augustus McBride opened the shade and looked out.

"It is himself. Augustus McBride!"

"The prophecy has come true at last."

But as the villagers surged to the carriage, Ethan stood alone, puzzled. He saw a wizened face, a face shrunken — as if in all his grasping Augustus McBride had himself been grasped and wrung out. When he reached from the carriage to drop copper coins to the shouting villagers, his fingers were curved into a claw.

No one but Ethan noticed this. The villagers followed Augustus McBride's dust to escort the great man to his mansion. Their cries echoed back: "The Great Stone Face has come at last!"

Ethan looked up to the mountain and then turned to his own home.

Years went by. Augustus McBride died not long after his wealth had disappeared. Now the villagers said that the wizened face of the ruined merchant had never matched the gentle majesty of the Great Stone Face.

Ethan had his own farm, and day by day he worked the land with tender hands curving furrows around the hillsides, lugging stones to walls, carrying water during drought, sharing his plenty during harvest. At dusk he sat on his porch, weary, and watched the glow on the Great Stone Face.

The village had grown larger. Its Main Street boasted a line of brick and clapboard houses, as well as a stone courthouse. Each spring the villagers met there to decide the town's course for the next year, and many a soul waited to hear what Ethan said before they made up their own minds. He would stand, his face thoughtful, and pause a moment before speaking. Then with deep and rumbling words, he spoke wisdom and peace.

One summer, when the Great Stone Face showed white with the heat, word came that stirred the village again. Years ago, one of the villagers had marched away to fight in the wars, and he had become Old Blood and Thunder, a great general. Now, hobbled by old wounds and weary of rolling drums, he was returning to the village.

Those who had known him as a boy swore that he had looked so like the Great Stone Face even then that he must be the fulfillment of the prophecy. When the general's aide, traveling through the village, was struck by how the Face resembled his commander, all were sure that the prophecy had come true.

The general arrived in a black coach, and the villagers so crowded around him that Ethan could not see his face. At the Common, a platform had been erected with flags and bunting. There the great man sat down to a banquet in his honor.

"It is the same face to a hair!" cried one of the villagers.

"Why, the Great Stone Face is nothing but Old Blood and Thunder himself on the mountain!"

Ethan felt the Great Stone Face's eyes upon the village, and he knew that they were especially watching Old Blood and Thunder.

The crowd hushed as the great man stood to speak. Ethan saw the sparkle of epaulets, and then, straining to his tiptoes, he saw the general's face.

It was not what the villagers had claimed. Here was a face war-worn and stern. None of the gentle wisdom that shone from the Great Stone Face was there.

"This is not the man," sighed Ethan, and he made his way out of the crowd.

More years sped quietly away. While Old Blood and Thunder rushed to new slaughters, Ethan married and had more children than he could hold at once. He watched his village grow into a town, cultivated his land to fertile harvests, built a home with his wife and houses with his neighbors, sorrowed and laughed with all he knew. His life was a stream that watered wide green banks all along its course, and every soul in the town who saw him smiled.

Ethan did not see the smiles. He went his way, children — his own and others — hanging off him, stopping at the Common to speak with old Pastor Hooper, pausing at the town well to take a cold drink with a neighbor, and turning in to the Dry Goods Store to read the gazettes up from Boston.

One wintry day, when cold sunlight fell on the frozen ground, Ethan read that Trumbell Bounderby was coming to the town. Like Augustus McBride and Old Blood and Thunder, Trumbell Bounderby had lived in the valley under the Great Stone Face. He too left, not to gather gold or to win wars, but to become a name. And he had done it. Crowds listened to him, whether he spoke sweetly of peace or sternly of war. He blustered on many a local Common, in halls of state, across the country, and even in Europe. His listeners marveled at his words that floated like a bright fog.

The banquet for Old Blood and Thunder was nothing compared to the festival planned for Trumbell Bounderby. Banners flew from every house, and portraits of the Great Stone Face smiling at Trumbell Bounderby were printed and set up in every store window.

Everyone gathered at the railroad tracks to greet the great man, and as the train clamored into the station a band began to play brassily. When Trumbull Bounderby himself appeared at the head of the steps, his face held a smile.

"There! There! Look at Trumbull Bounderby and see if he is not the Great Stone Face."

"The Great Stone Face has met his match at last!"

As Ethan looked at the smiling man, he did see something of the old familiar face on the mountain. There was the strength, but in Trumbull Bounderby Ethan saw a man who performed for airy fame.

"Confess it! Is he not the very image of the Great Stone Face?"

"Neighbor," answered Ethan, "I see no real likeness." And he turned away.

Years hurried on. When he lived past his fame, Trumbull Bounderby grew bitter and sailed back to Europe. Ethan's children took farms of their own, sowing and harvesting with the same tender hands of their father. The years planted white hairs on Ethan's head and furrowed his cheeks with wrinkles. But his eyes did not change; he watched his children and his children's children with love.

One day, close to sunset, Ethan sat under the freshly-green maples of the Common with his neighbors and the ancient Pastor Hooper. They spoke of long winters and blooming springs, of tasks started and finished. When Ethan's granddaughter came to fetch him home for supper, talk had turned to the prophecy of the Great Stone Face.

"I'm afraid," said Pastor Hooper, "after all these years, I'll not see the prophecy fulfilled."

"Well," said Ethan, drawing his granddaughter to him, "perhaps this one will see it come to pass."

"But, Grandfather," she said, "the prophecy came true long ago."

"What do you mean, child?" asked Pastor Hooper.

Ethan's granddaughter reached two slight fingers to her grandfather's face. She traced the arch of his rugged brow, the hollows of his eyes, the furrows of his cheeks, and then stopped her fingers tenderly on his lips.

Sudden silence on the Common. Some of the neighbors stood.

"The child has seen deeper than all of us," whispered Pastor Hooper.

Then all the townspeople looked, and they knew the truth.

But Ethan smiled, shook his head, and taking the hand of his granddaughter, walked homeward.